GCSE English AQA Anthology

The Workbook

Poems from Different Cultures

AQA A Specification — Higher Level

This book is for anyone doing GCSE AQA Anthology at Higher Level.

It contains lots of tricky questions designed to hone your poetry skills — because that's the only way you'll get any better.

It's also got some daft bits in to try and make the whole experience at least vaguely entertaining for you.

What CGP is all about

Our sole aim here at CGP is to produce the highest quality books — carefully written, immaculately presented and dangerously close to being funny.

Then we work our socks off to get them out to you — at the cheapest possible prices.

Edward Kamau Brathwaite

Edward Kamau Brathwaite was born in 1930 in Barbados in the West Indies. He's a poet and historian, and he's interested in links between slave nations and their African origins.

Limbo

And limbo stick is the silence in front of me
limbo

limbo
limbo like me
limbo
limbo like me

long dark night is the silence in front of me
limbo
limbo like me

stick hit sound
and the ship like it ready

stick hit sound
and the dark still steady

limbo
limbo like me

long dark deck and the water surrounding me
long dark deck and the silence is over me

limbo
limbo like me

stick is the whip
and the dark deck is slavery

stick is the whip
and the dark deck is slavery

limbo
limbo like me

drum stick knock
and the darkness is over me

knees spread wide
and the water is hiding

limbo
limbo like me

knees spread wide
and the dark ground is under me

down
down
down

and the drummer is calling me

limbo
limbo like me

sun coming up
and the drummers are praising me

out of the dark
and the dumb gods are raising me

up
up
up

and the music is saving me

hot
slow
step

on the burning ground.

POEM DICTIONARY

Limbo has several meanings —

1. The West Indian dance, crouching backwards to pass under a horizontal stick — said to have originated from the experience of moving round in the cramped decks of the slave ships
2. An imaginary place for the unwanted or forgotten
3. In Christianity, a place where the souls of infants who die before baptism go

Limbo

Q1 What does the phrase "knees spread wide" tell you about the conditions on the ship?

....

....

Q2 Give an example of visual imagery in the poem.

....

....

Q3 What is the effect of the rhythm of lines 10 and 12?

....

....

....

Q4 a) Why do you think the poet repeats the lines "*limbo, limbo like me*"?

....

....

....

b) Find another example of repetition in the poem and describe the effect it has.

....

....

....

Q5 Pick out a phrase from the poem which stands out to you. Explain why it is significant in the poem.

....

....

....

....

Tatamkhulu Afrika

Tatamkhulu Afrika was born in Egypt in 1920 but raised as a white South African in District Six of Cape Town. When apartheid was introduced, he refused to be classed as a "superior" white. He joined the African National Congress (ANC) and was a political prisoner because of his fight against apartheid.

Nothing's Changed

Small round hard stones click
under my heels,
seeding grasses thrust
bearded seeds
into trouser cuffs, cans,
trodden on, crunch
in tall, purple-flowering,
amiable weeds.

District Six.
No board says it is:
but my feet know,
and my hands,
and the skin about my bones,
and the soft labouring of my lungs,
and the hot, white, inwards turning
anger of my eyes.

Brash with glass,
name flaring like a flag,
it squats
in the grass and weeds,
incipient Port Jackson trees:
new, up-market, haute cuisine,
guard at the gatepost,
whites only inn.

No sign says it is:
but we know where we belong.

I press my nose
to the clear panes, know,
before I see them, there will be
crushed ice white glass,
linen falls,
the single rose.

Down the road,
working man's cafe sells
bunny chows.
Take it with you, eat
it at a plastic table's top,
wipe your fingers on your jeans,
spit a little on the floor:
it's in the bone.

I back from the glass,
boy again,
leaving small mean O
of small, mean mouth.
Hands burn
for a stone, a bomb,
to shiver down the glass.
Nothing's changed.

POEM DICTIONARY
amiable — likeable / friendly
incipient — developing, just starting
Port Jackson trees — large pine trees
haute cuisine — high-class, expensive food
bunny chows — cheap food for the poor

Nothing's Changed

Q1 What impression do we get of District Six from the descriptions in the first verse? What words give you this impression?

....

....

....

Q2 Complete the table below with phrases from the poem which show how the inn and the cafe differ.

	The inn	The cafe
Type of food		
Eating surface		
Hygiene/cleanliness		

Q3 What effect do lines 10 and 25 have?

....

....

....

Q4 Why does the poet want to act violently at the end of the poem?

....

....

....

....

Q5 Now choose a phrase from the poem which stands out to you. Explain why you like or dislike it.

....

....

....

....

Grace Nichols

Grace Nichols was born in Guyana in 1950. She was a journalist in the Caribbean until she moved to Britain in 1977. Both of these cultures and how they interlink are important to her.

Island Man

(for a Caribbean island man in London who
still wakes up to the sound of the sea)

Morning
and island man wakes up
to the sound of blue surf
in his head
the steady breaking and wombing

wild seabirds
and fishermen pushing out to sea
the sun surfacing defiantly
from the east
of his small emerald island
he always comes back   groggily groggily

Comes back to sands
of a grey metallic soar
                    to surge of wheels
to dull North Circular roar

muffling muffling
his crumpled pillow waves
island man heaves himself

Another London day

POEM DICTIONARY
North Circular — a busy London road

Island Man

Q1 Find two phrases from the poem, one about the Caribbean and one about London, which show their contrasting colours.

Caribbean 'emerald island' ....

London 'grey metallic soar' ....

Q2 Which phrase is repeated on different lines to show that the man is gradually returning to reality?

....

Q3 How does the poet create the effect of being in a dream?

....

....

....

Q4 What is the effect of the unusual layout on lines 11 and 14?

....

....

....

....

Q5 How do you think the man feels at the end of the poem? Give a relevant quote.

....

....

....

....

Q6 Now select a phrase from the poem which you can relate to and explain why you chose it.

....

....

....

....

Imtiaz Dharker

<u>Imtiaz Dharker</u> was born in Pakistan in 1954, and brought up as a Muslim in Glasgow. She now lives in India, with her husband who is Indian and a Hindu. She feels that identity is to do with "beliefs and states of mind", rather than nationality or religion.

Blessing

The skin cracks like a pod.
There never is enough water.

Imagine the drip of it,
the small splash, echo
in a tin mug,
the voice of a kindly god.

Sometimes, the sudden rush
of fortune. The municipal pipe bursts,
silver crashes to the ground
and the flow has found
a roar of tongues. From the huts,
a congregation: every man woman
child for streets around
butts in, with pots,
brass, copper, aluminium,
plastic buckets,
frantic hands,

and naked children
screaming in the liquid sun,
their highlights polished to perfection,
flashing light,
as the blessing sings
over their small bones.

<u>POEM DICTIONARY</u>
municipal — to do with the city

Blessing

Q1 Write down three words in the poem which create a religious feel.

i) .... ii) .... iii) ....

Q2 Find a phrase from the poem which suggests:

a) a sense of urgency. ....

b) that a miracle has happened. ....

Q3 How do you know that water is very precious to the people in the poem? Use a quote from the poem in your answer.

....

....

Q4 What impression do lines 1-6 give us of everyday life for the people in the poem? Support your answer with a relevant quote.

....

....

....

....

Q5 What is the effect of the descriptions of the items the people use to collect the water?

....

....

....

....

Q6 Now you're familiar with the poem, choose a phrase which stands out to you. Then explain why you like or dislike it.

....

....

....

....

Lawrence Ferlinghetti

Lawrence Ferlinghetti was born in New York in 1919. He settled in San Francisco and is interested in how different cultures and races mix. He's concerned about the growing gap between rich and poor.

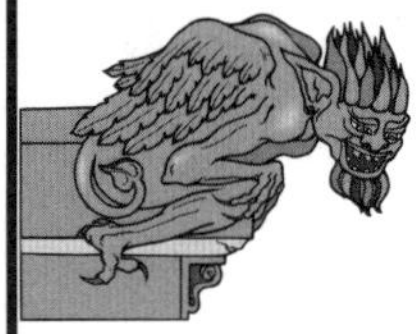

Two Scavengers in a Truck,
Two Beautiful People in a Mercedes

At the stoplight waiting for the light
nine a.m. downtown San Francisco
a bright yellow garbage truck
with two garbagemen in red plastic blazers
standing on the back stoop
one on each side hanging on
and looking down into
an elegant open Mercedes
with an elegant couple in it
The man
in a hip three-piece linen suit
with shoulder-length blond hair & sunglasses
The young blond woman so casually coifed
with a short skirt and colored stockings
on the way to his architect's office

And the two scavengers up since four a.m.
grungy from their route
on the way home
The older of the two with grey iron hair
and hunched back
looking down like some
gargoyle Quasimodo
And the younger of the two
also with sunglasses & long hair
about the same age as the Mercedes driver

And both scavengers gazing down
as from a great distance
at the cool couple
as if they were watching some odorless TV ad
in which everything is always possible

And the very red light for an instant
holding all four close together
as if anything at all were possible
between them
across that small gulf
in the high seas
of this democracy

POEM DICTIONARY

stoop — rear footplate of a truck
coifed — stylishly arranged hair
Quasimodo — the fictional hunchbacked bell ringer of Notre Dame
hip — fashionable
gargoyle — a carved monster on a church wall
odorless — with no smell (American spelling)

Two Scavengers in a Truck, Two Beautiful People in a Mercedes

Q1 There are loads of contrasts in this poem. Fill in the table below using words from the poem.

	The Scavengers	The Beautiful People
Their job		
Their transport		
Their hair		
Their clothes		

Q2 Write down three words in the poem which make you think of American culture and language.

i) .... ii) .... iii) ....

Q3 Why do you think the poet has chosen not to use any full stops?

....

....

Q4 What do you think the poet's attitude towards the beautiful couple in the Mercedes is? Support your answer with a quote from the poem.

....

....

....

....

Q5 OK, like you've done before, pick out a phrase from the poem and explain why you like or dislike it.

....

....

....

....

Nissim Ezekiel

Nissim Ezekiel was born in Bombay in 1924, to Jewish parents. But he was raised in a mainly Hindu culture, and has been influenced by atheist views.

Night of the Scorpion

I remember the night my mother
was stung by a scorpion. Ten hours
of steady rain had driven him
to crawl beneath a sack of rice.
Parting with his poison – flash
of diabolic tail in the dark room –
he risked the rain again.
The peasants came like swarms of flies
and buzzed the name of God a hundred times
to paralyse the Evil One.
With candles and with lanterns
throwing giant scorpion shadows
on the mud-baked walls
they searched for him: he was not found.
They clicked their tongues.
With every movement that the scorpion made
his poison moved in Mother's blood, they said.
May he sit still, they said.
May the sins of your previous birth
be burned away tonight, they said.
May your suffering decrease
the misfortunes of your next birth, they said.
May the sum of evil
balanced in this unreal world
against the sum of good
become diminished by your pain.
May the poison purify your flesh
of desire, and your spirit of ambition,
they said, and they sat around
on the floor with my mother in the centre,
the peace of understanding on each face.
More candles, more lanterns, more neighbours,
more insects, and the endless rain.
My mother twisted through and through,
groaning on a mat.
My father, sceptic, rationalist,
trying every curse and blessing,
powder, mixture, herb and hybrid.
He even poured a little paraffin
upon the bitten toe and put a match to it.
I watched the flame feeding on my mother.
I watched the holy man perform his rites
to tame the poison with an incantation.
After twenty hours
it lost its sting.

My mother only said
Thank God the scorpion picked on me
and spared my children.

POEM DICTIONARY
diabolic — to do with the devil
diminished — reduced
sceptic — a doubtful person
rationalist — a person who uses logical thinking to explain things
hybrid — a mixture of things
rites — actions in a ceremony
incantation — religious chanting

Night of the Scorpion

Q1 Write down a phrase from the poem which shows that:

a) the poet's mother is in pain.

....

b) the villagers associate the scorpion with the devil.

....

Q2 Pick out one idea from the Hindu religion which is mentioned in the poem.

....

....

Q3 Why do you think the author has chosen to write the poem from the perspective of a child?

....

....

Q4 What is the effect of the poet describing his father as a "sceptic" (line 36)?

....

....

....

Q5 What do you think is the poet's attitude towards the neighbours' religious response? Support your answer with a quote.

....

....

....

....

Q6 Read through the poem again and write down the phrase that stands out the most to you. Explain why you like or dislike the phrase.

....

....

....

....

Chinua Achebe

Chinua Achebe was born in Nigeria in 1930. He worked for the Nigerian Broadcasting Corporation, but when war broke out in 1967, he joined the government of Biafra (the area that violently split from the rest of Nigeria). He's written lots of poems about war and its effects.

Vultures

In the greyness
and drizzle of one despondent
dawn unstirred by harbingers
of sunbreak a vulture
perching high on broken
bone of a dead tree
nestled close to his
mate his smooth
bashed-in head, a pebble
on a stem rooted in
a dump of gross
feathers, inclined affectionately
to hers. Yesterday they picked
the eyes of a swollen
corpse in a water-logged
trench and ate the
things in its bowel. Full
gorged they chose their roost
keeping the hollowed remnant
in easy range of cold
telescopic eyes ...
Strange
indeed how love in other
ways so particular
will pick a corner
in that charnel-house
tidy it and coil up there, perhaps
even fall asleep – her face
turned to the wall!
... Thus the Commandant at Belsen
Camp going home for
the day with fumes of
human roast clinging
rebelliously to his hairy
nostrils will stop
at the wayside sweet-shop
and pick up a chocolate
for his tender offspring
waiting at home for Daddy's
return...
Praise bounteous
providence if you will
that grants even an ogre
a tiny glow-worm
tenderness encapsulated
in icy caverns of a cruel
heart or else despair
for in the very germ
of that kindred love is
lodged the perpetuity
of evil.

POEM DICTIONARY

harbinger — a messenger / a sign of things to come
charnel-house — a place where corpses are stored
Commandant — a commanding officer
Belsen — a Nazi concentration camp
bounteous providence — the good things that God has given to mankind
encapsulated — enclosed
perpetuity — lasting forever

Vultures

Q1 Fill in the table below with phrases from the poem that describe the different qualities of the vultures and the Commandant.

	The vultures	The Commandant
Ugliness		
Evil		
Kindness		

Q2 What effect does the phrase "if you will" (line 42) have?

....

....

Q3 Explain how the poet creates a solemn mood in the poem. Use quotes from the poem in your answer.

....

....

....

....

Q4 What connection does the poet see between the vultures and the Commandant?

....

....

....

....

Q5 No surprise here — pick out a phrase from the poem which stands out to you. Explain why you like or dislike it.

....

....

....

....

Denise Levertov

Denise Levertov (1923-97) was born in England but moved to New York in 1947. She later became an American citizen, but was strongly opposed to the USA's involvement in the Vietnam War.

What Were They Like?

1) Did the people of Viet Nam
use lanterns of stone?
2) Did they hold ceremonies
to reverence the opening of buds?
3) Were they inclined to quiet laughter?
4) Did they use bone and ivory,
jade and silver, for ornament?
5) Had they an epic poem?
6) Did they distinguish between speech and singing?

1) Sir, their light hearts turned to stone.
It is not remembered whether in gardens
stone lanterns illumined pleasant ways.
2) Perhaps they gathered once to delight in blossom,
but after the children were killed
there were no more buds)
3) Sir, laughter is bitter to the burned mouth.
4) A dream ago, perhaps. Ornament is for joy.
All the bones were charred.
5) It is not remembered. Remember,
most were peasants; their life
was in rice and bamboo.
When peaceful clouds were reflected in the paddies
and the water buffalo stepped surely along terraces,
maybe fathers told their sons old tales.
When bombs smashed those mirrors
there was time only to scream.
6) There is an echo yet
of their speech which was like a song.
It was reported that their singing resembled
the flight of moths in moonlight.
Who can say? It is silent now.

POEM DICTIONARY

reverence — deep respect or worship
jade — a gemstone, normally green
illumined — lit up
charred — blackened by fire
paddies — waterlogged fields for growing rice
terraces — different levels of fields for farming

What Were They Like?

Q1 What form does this poem take? Suggest a reason why the author chose this style.

....

....

....

....

Q2 Find a word which has different meanings in different parts of the poem and explain how its meaning changes.

....

....

....

Q3 How is the Vietnamese language described?
Use a quote from the poem to back up your answer.

....

....

....

Q4 What impression does the poem give us of the Vietnamese way of life before the war?
Explain your answer with a relevant quote.

....

....

....

Q5 It's time for you to pick out a phrase. Don't forget to explain how it makes you feel.

....

....

....

....

Sujata Bhatt

<u>Sujata Bhatt</u> was born in India in 1956, later lived in the USA and now lives in Germany with her husband. She writes in both English and Gujarati, her mother tongue.

from Search For My Tongue

You ask me what I mean
by saying I have lost my tongue.
I ask you, what would you do
if you had two tongues in your mouth,
and lost the first one, the mother tongue,
and could not really know the other,
the foreign tongue.
You could not use them both together
even if you thought that way.
And if you lived in a place you had to
speak a foreign tongue,
your mother tongue would rot,
rot and die in your mouth
until you had to spit it out.
I thought I spit it out
but overnight while I dream,
મને હતું કે આખ્ખી જીભ આખ્ખી ભાષા,
(munay hutoo kay aakhee jeebh aakhee bhasha)
મેં થૂંકી નાખી છે.
(may thoonky nakhi chay)
પરંતુ રાત્રે સ્વપ્નામાં મારી ભાષા પાછી આવે છે.
(parantoo rattray svupnama mari bhasha pachi aavay chay)
ફુલની જેમ મારી ભાષા મારી જીભ
(foolnee jaim mari bhasha mari jeebh)
મોઢામાં ખીલે છે.
(modhama kheelay chay)
ફળની જેમ મારી ભાષા મારી જીભ
(fullnee jaim mari bhasha mari jeebh)
મોઢામાં પાકે છે.
(modhama pakay chay)
it grows back, a stump of a shoot
grows longer, grows moist, grows strong veins,
it ties the other tongue in knots,
the bud opens, the bud opens in my mouth,
it pushes the other tongue aside.
Everytime I think I've forgotten,
I think I've lost the mother tongue,
it blossoms out of my mouth.

<u>POEM DICTIONARY</u>
mother tongue — a person's first language

Search For My Tongue

Q1 What effect does the inclusion of Gujarati words have on the visual appearance of the poem?

....

....

Q2 a) What metaphor does the poet use to represent her mother tongue?

....

....

b) What effect do you think the poet is trying to create by using this metaphor?

....

....

....

Q3 Why do you think the poet uses the words "you" and "I" a lot?

....

....

....

Q4 In lines 17-30, we "hear" the Gujarati language. How important do you think this is to the impact of the poem? Explain your answer.

....

....

....

Q5 Now choose a phrase from the poem which appeals to you and explain why you like or dislike it.

....

....

....

....

Tom Leonard

Tom Leonard was born in Glasgow in 1944. He's often written about people's attitudes to different accents, and says he writes in Scottish dialect so that his 'voice' can be heard through his poetry.

from **Unrelated Incidents**

this is thi
six a clock
news thi
man said n
thi reason
a talk wia
BBC accent
iz coz yi
widny wahnt
mi ti talk
aboot thi
trooth wia
voice lik
wanna yoo
scruff. if
a toktaboot
thi trooth
lik wanna yoo
scruff yi
widny thingk
it wuz troo.
jist wanna yoo
scruff tokn.
thirza right
way ti spell
ana right way
ti tok it. this
is me tokn yir
right way a
spellin. this
is ma trooth
yooz doant no
thi trooth
yirsellz cawz
yi canny talk
right. this is
the six a clock
nyooz. belt up.

Unrelated Incidents

Q1 Which repeated phrase suggests the newsreader looks down on working-class people?

....

Q2 Re-write these phrases from the poem into standard English.

a) "yi widny thingk it wuz troo"

....

b) "thirza right way ti spell ana right way ti tok it"

....

c) "yooz doant no thi trooth yirsellz"

....

Q3 What is meant by the phrase "BBC accent"?

....

Q4 Why does the newsreader believe that the news shouldn't be read in a regional accent? Support your answer with a quote.

....

....

....

Q5 Why do you think the poet has chosen to put the newsreader's attitude into Scottish dialect?

....

....

....

Q6 Choose a phrase from the poem that you find interesting. Explain why you chose it.

....

....

....

....

John Agard

John Agard was born in Guyana in South America in 1949, to parents of mixed nationality. He came to Britain in 1977. He likes to perform his poems, and believes humour is an effective way of challenging people's opinions.

Half-Caste

Excuse me
standing on one leg
I'm half-caste

Explain yuself
wha yu mean
when yu say half-caste
yu mean when picasso
mix red an green
is a half-caste canvas/
explain yuself
wha yu mean
when yu say half-caste
yu mean when light an shadow
mix in de sky
is a half-caste weather/
well in dat case
england weather
nearly always half-caste
in fact some o dem cloud
half-caste till dem overcast
so spiteful dem dont want de sun pass
ah rass/
explain yuself
wha yu mean
when yu say half-caste
yu mean tchaikovsky
sit down at dah piano
an mix a black key
wid a white key
is a half-caste symphony/

Explain yuself
wha yu mean
Ah listening to yu wid de keen
half of mih ear
Ah lookin at yu wid de keen
half of mih eye
and when I'm introduced to yu
I'm sure you'll understand
why I offer yu half-a-hand
an when I sleep at night
I close half-a-eye
consequently when I dream
I dream half-a-dream
an when moon begin to glow
I half-caste human being
cast half-a-shadow
but yu must come back tomorrow
wid de whole of yu eye
an de whole of yu ear
an de whole of yu mind

an I will tell yu
de other half
of my story

POEM DICTIONARY
Picasso — the name of a 20th Century Spanish painter
Tchaikovsky — the name of a 19th Century Russian classical music composer

Half-Caste

Q1 Give two examples of natural imagery used in the poem.

i) ....

ii) ....

Q2 At the end of the poem (lines 47-53) what does the poet say people must do before he will tell them "de other half" of his story? Explain what he means in your own words.

....

....

....

Q3 How does the poet use humour to make his point? Support your answer with a quote.

....

....

....

....

Q4 How does the poet create an argumentative tone? Include quotes in your answer.

....

....

....

....

Q5 Which phrase in the poem stands out to you the most? Explain why you like or dislike it.

....

....

....

....

Derek Walcott

Derek Walcott was born in St Lucia, in the West Indies, in 1930. His father was English and his mother was African. As well as poetry, he's written plays, and is a painter.

Love After Love

The time will come
When, with elation,
You will greet yourself arriving
At your own door, in your own mirror,
And each will smile at the other's welcome,

And say sit here. Eat.
You will love again the stranger who was your self.
Give wine. Give bread. Give back your heart
To itself, to the stranger who has loved you

All your life, whom you ignored
For another, who knows you by heart.
Take down the love-letters from the bookshelf

The photographs, the desperate notes,
Peel your own images from the mirror.
Sit. Feast on your life.

POEM DICTIONARY
elation — an extreme feeling of joy

Love After Love

Q1 Give two examples of religious / ceremonial language in the poem.

i)..

ii)..

Q2 Who is the "stranger" that the poet talks about?

....

....

Q3 What advice does the poet give to the reader? Use a quote from the poem in your answer.

....

....

....

Q4 Why does the poet advise the reader to take down their love-letters and photographs?

....

....

....

Q5 Does the poet think solitary life is a good or bad thing? Support your answer with a quote.

....

....

....

....

Q6 Now explain why you like or dislike one phrase which stands out to you in the poem.

....

....

....

....

Imtiaz Dharker

Imtiaz Dharker was born in Pakistan in 1954. She has said that she believes identity comes from "beliefs and states of mind", rather than nationality or religion.

This Room

This room is breaking out
of itself, cracking through
its own walls
in search of space, light,
empty air.

The bed is lifting out of
its nightmares.
From dark corners, chairs
are rising up to crash through clouds.

This is the time and place
to be alive:
when the daily furniture of our lives
stirs, when the improbable arrives.
Pots and pans bang together
in celebration, clang
past the crowd of garlic, onions, spices,
fly by the ceiling fan.
No one is looking for the door.

In all this excitement
I'm wondering where
I've left my feet, and why

my hands are outside, clapping.

This Room

Q1 Write down three examples of onomatopoeia from the poem.

i) ....

ii) ....

iii) ....

Q2 Make a list of objects that are personified in this poem.

....

....

....

Q3 Write down one example of metaphorical language in the poem and describe what effect it has.

Metaphor ....

Effect ....

....

....

Q4 How do you think the poet feels about what is happening? Support your answer with a quote.

....

....

....

....

Q5 Choose a phrase from the poem that interests you — explain why you chose it.

....

....

....

....

Moniza Alvi

Moniza Alvi was born in Pakistan in 1954, to a Pakistani father and an English mother. She moved to England as a child, and revisited Pakistan for the first time in 1993.

Presents from my Aunts in Pakistan

They sent me a salwar kameez
peacock-blue,
and another
glistening like an orange split open,
embossed slippers, gold and black
points curling.
Candy-striped glass bangles
snapped, drew blood.
Like at school, fashions changed
in Pakistan –
the salwar bottoms were broad and stiff,
then narrow.
My aunts chose an apple-green sari,
silver-bordered
for my teens.

I tried each satin-silken top –
was alien in the sitting-room.
I could never be as lovely
as those clothes –
I longed
for denim and corduroy.
My costume clung to me
and I was aflame,
I couldn't rise up out of its fire,
half-English,
unlike Aunt Jamila.

I wanted my parents' camel-skin lamp –
switching it on in my bedroom,
to consider the cruelty
and the transformation
from camel to shade,
marvel at the colours
like stained glass.

My mother cherished her jewellery –
Indian gold, dangling, filigree.
But it was stolen from our car.
The presents were radiant in my wardrobe.
My aunts requested cardigans
from Marks and Spencers.

My salwar kameez
didn't impress the schoolfriend
who sat on my bed, asked to see
my weekend clothes.
But often I admired the mirror-work,
tried to glimpse myself
in the miniature
glass circles, recall the story
how the three of us
sailed to England.
Prickly heat had me screaming on the way.
I ended up in a cot
in my English grandmother's dining-room,
found myself alone,
playing with a tin boat.

I pictured my birthplace
from fifties' photographs.
When I was older
there was conflict, a fractured land
throbbing through newsprint.
Sometimes I saw Lahore –
my aunts in shaded rooms,
screened from male visitors,
sorting presents,
wrapping them in tissue.

Or there were beggars, sweeper-girls
and I was there –
of no fixed nationality,
staring through fretwork
at the Shalimar Gardens.

POEM DICTIONARY

salwar kameez — a Pakistani item of clothing
Lahore — a city in Pakistan
filigree — delicate gold jewellery
Shalimar Gardens — peaceful, walled gardens in Lahore

Presents from my Aunts in Pakistan

Q1 a) Write down three words in the poem which suggest a negative image of Pakistan.

i) .... ii) .... iii) ....

b) Write down three words in the poem which describe the clothes from Pakistan in an admiring way.

i) .... ii) .... iii) ....

Q2 Explain what you think the following phrases mean:

a) "Was alien in the sitting room"

....

....

....

b) "I admired the mirror-work, tried to glimpse myself in the miniature glass circles".

....

....

....

Q3 How clear are the poet's memories of Pakistan? Explain your answer.

....

....

....

Q4 How does the poet feel about her identity at the end of the poem? Support your answer with a quote.

....

....

....

Q5 Write down a phrase from the poem that grabs your attention.
Briefly explain why you like or dislike it.

....

....

....

Niyi Osundare

Niyi Osundare was born in Nigeria in 1947, and is a Professor of English. He has often spoken out against military regimes in his home country.

Not my Business

They picked Akanni up one morning
Beat him soft like clay
And stuffed him down the belly
Of a waiting jeep.
    What business of mine is it
    So long they don't take the yam
    From my savouring mouth?

They came one night
Booted the whole house awake
And dragged Danladi out,
Then off to a lengthy absence.
    What business of mine is it
    So long they don't take the yam
    From my savouring mouth?

Chinwe went to work one day
Only to find her job was gone:
No query, no warning, no probe –
Just one neat sack for a stainless record.
    What business of mine is it
    So long they don't take the yam
    From my savouring mouth?

And then one evening
As I sat down to eat my yam
A knock on the door froze my hungry hand.
The jeep was waiting on my bewildered lawn
Waiting, waiting in its usual silence.

POEM DICTIONARY
yam — vegetable eaten in hot countries

Not my Business

Q1 What poetic device does the author use to describe the jeep and the lawn?

....

Q2 Why is the title of the poem ironic?

....

....

....

Q3 Why do you think the poet:

a) mentions the time of day in the first line of each verse?

....

....

b) describes the victims by their first names?

....

....

Q4 What is the effect of the three lines that are repeated?

....

....

....

....

Q5 Look over the poem again and pick out the phrase that stands out to you most. Explain what effect they have on you.

....

....

....

....

Grace Nichols

Grace Nichols was born in Guyana in 1950. She now lives and writes in Sussex.

Hurricane Hits England

It took a hurricane, to bring her closer
To the landscape.
Half the night she lay awake,
The howling ship of the wind,
Its gathering rage,
Like some dark ancestral spectre.
Fearful and reassuring.

Talk to me Huracan
Talk to me Oya
Talk to me Shango
And Hattie,
My sweeping, back-home cousin.

Tell me why you visit
An English coast?
What is the meaning
Of old tongues
Reaping havoc
In new places?

The blinding illumination,
Even as you short-
Circuit us
Into further darkness?

What is the meaning of trees
Falling heavy as whales
Their crusted roots
Their cratered graves?

O why is my heart unchained?

Tropical Oya of the Weather,
I am aligning myself to you,
I am following the movement of your winds,
I am riding the mystery of your storm.

Ah, sweet mystery,
Come to break the frozen lake in me,
Shaking the foundations of the very trees within me,
Come to let me know
That the earth is the earth is the earth.

Hurricane Hits England

Q1 In your own words, write a summary of what happens in the poem.

....

....

....

....

Q2 What real-life event is the poem based on?

....

Q3 What are Oya, Huracan and Shango?

....

....

Q4 How has the character in the poem been feeling before the storm? Use a quotation in your answer.

....

....

....

....

Q5 What do you think the last line of the poem means?

....

....

....

Q6 For one last time — choose a phrase that stands out to you in the poem and explain why you like or dislike it.

....

....

....

....

Identity

These Poems are about Identity:

Limbo (pages 2-3)
Nothing's Changed (pages 4-5)
Island Man (pages 6-7)
Search For My Tongue (pages 18-19)
Unrelated Incidents (pages 20-21)
Half-Caste (pages 22-23)
Love After Love (pages 24-25)
This Room (pages 26-27)
Presents from my Aunts in Pakistan (pages 28-29)
Hurricane Hits England (pages 32-33)

Q1 Write a couple of sentences about your identity.

....

....

....

....

Q2 Choose a poem that you know from the top of the page.
What does this poem say about the way people think of themselves?

....

....

....

....

....

Q3 Pick another poem that you know, from the list at the top of the page.
What does this poem say about how people view others?

....

....

....

....

....

EXAM-STYLE QUESTION Q4 Compare how the poets present their ideas about identity in 'Nothing's Changed' and one other poem.

EXAM-STYLE QUESTION Q5 In 'Love After Love', we see how a return to the true self is a cause of celebration.
Compare this to one other poem that is concerned with identity.

Politics

These Poems are about Politics:

Nothing's Changed (pages 4-5)
Two Scavengers in a Truck... (pages 10-11)
Vultures (pages 14-15)
What Were They Like? (pages 16-17)
Unrelated Incidents (pages 20-21)
Not my Business (pages 30-31)

Q1 If you were to write a poem about a political issue, which issue would you choose, and why?

....

....

....

....

Q2 Choose a poem from the top of the page that you know well.
What political situation does the poet describe, and what is his / her attitude towards it?

....

....

....

....

....

Q3 Choose a different poem. What is the poet's political viewpoint in this poem?

....

....

....

....

....

EXAM-STYLE QUESTION

Q4 Divisions in society are described in 'Two Scavengers in a Truck...'
Choose one other poem with a political theme and compare how the poets present their ideas.

EXAM-STYLE QUESTION

Q5 The mistreatment of individuals in society is described in 'Not my Business'.
Compare this with one other poem which has a political theme.

Change

These Poems are about Change:

Nothing's Changed (pages 4-5)
Blessing (pages 8-9)
What Were They Like? (pages 16-17)
Search For My Tongue (pages 18-19)
Love After Love (pages 24-25)
This Room (pages 26-27)
Presents from my Aunts in Pakistan (pages 28-29)
Hurricane Hits England (pages 32-33)

Q1 Write a couple of sentences about a change that has happened in your life.

....

....

....

....

Q2 Choose a poem that you know from the top of the page.
What kind of change does this poem describe?

....

....

....

....

....

Q3 Choose a different poem. Does the poet see change as a positive or a negative thing? Why?

....

....

....

....

....

EXAM-STYLE QUESTION Q4 The poet in 'Search For My Tongue' is concerned about changes in her life. Compare the view of change in this poem with the way change is presented in one other poem from the Poems from Different Cultures.

EXAM-STYLE QUESTION Q5 The poem 'What Were They Like?' addresses change in a community. Compare it with one other poem which deals with the theme of change.

People

These Poems are about People:

Island Man (pages 6-7)
Two Scavengers in a Truck... (pages 10-11)
Night of the Scorpion (pages 12-13)
Vultures (pages 14-15)
Search For My Tongue (pages 18-19)
Half-Caste (pages 22-23)
Presents from my Aunts in Pakistan (pages 28-29)
Not my Business (pages 30-31)
Hurricane Hits England (pages 32-33)

Q1 Write a paragraph about a person or people who are important to you.

....

....

....

....

Q2 Pick a poem from the top of the page that you know well.
What impression does the poet create of the person or people in this poem?

....

....

....

....

....

Q3 Choose a character or group of characters from a different poem.
How does this person / do these people interact with other people in society?

....

....

....

....

....

EXAM-STYLE QUESTION Q4 People's reactions to situations vary greatly. Compare 'Night of the Scorpion' to one other poem that shows people responding to a situation in which they find themselves.

EXAM-STYLE QUESTION Q5 In 'Not my Business', the poet encourages the reader to think about social responsibility. Compare this with one other poem that talks about how people relate to each other.

First Person

These Poems use the First Person:

Q1 Describe two reasons why you think a poet might decide to write in the first person.

i) ....

....

ii) ....

....

Q2 Yep, it's time for another of these questions — choose a poem that you know from the top of the page. How does using the first person make the poem's message more effective?

....

....

....

....

....

Q3 Choose a different poem. Why do you think the poet has chosen to use the first person in this poem?

....

....

....

....

....

EXAM-STYLE QUESTION Q4 Using the first person to present ideas can have certain advantages. Compare 'Presents from My Aunts...' with one other poem in the first person and explain how this device reinforces the poets' ideas.

EXAM-STYLE QUESTION Q5 In 'Night of the Scorpion' we see the incident through the eyes of a young child. Find one other poem that uses the first person and compare them.

Specific Cultural References

These Poems have Specific Cultural References:

Limbo (pages 2-3)
Nothing's Changed (pages 4-5)
Two Scavengers in a Truck... (pages 10-11)
Night of the Scorpion (pages 12-13)
What Were They Like? (pages 16-17)
Search For My Tongue (pages 18-19)
Presents from my Aunts in Pakistan (pages 30-31)
Not my Business (pages 28-29)
Hurricane Hits England (pages 32-33)

Q1 Describe a culture that you feel part of, or that you have experienced.

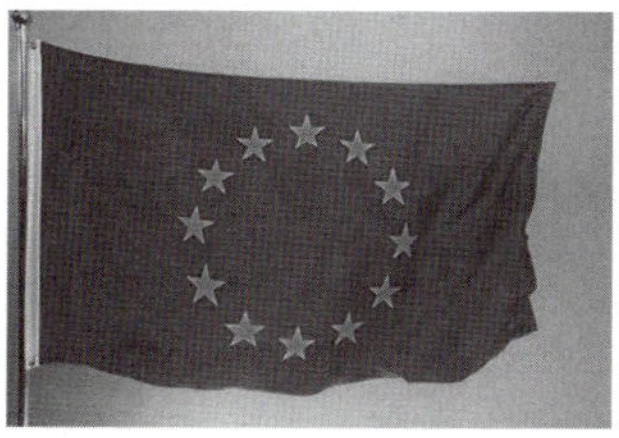

....

....

....

....

Q2 See those poems in the box at the top? Pick one.
In this poem, which culture does the poet describe, and what impression do we get of this culture?

....

....

....

....

....

Q3 Choose another poem from the box. How important to the poem's message is the culture described?

....

....

....

....

....

EXAM-STYLE QUESTION Q4 Some poems portray a certain culture or its customs. Compare 'What Were They Like?' to one other poem that uses specific cultural references.

EXAM-STYLE QUESTION Q5 Clothes are a specific cultural detail in 'Presents from My Aunts...'. Find one other poem that uses cultural details and compare how the poets use them.

Description

These Poems use Detailed Description:

Nothing's Changed (pages 4-5)
Island Man (pages 6-7)
Blessing (pages 8-9)
Two Scavengers in a Truck... (pages 10-11)
Night of the Scorpion (pages 12-13)
Vultures (pages 14-15)
Presents from my Aunts in Pakistan (pages 28-29)

Q1 Think about the funniest thing you've ever seen. Describe it in a brilliant and poetic way.

....

....

....

....

Q2 Pick a poem. A real beauty. One you know well. One from the box at the top of the page. How effective do you think the poet's use of description is?

....

....

....

....

....

Q3 Choose another poem. How do we get a sense of the poet's opinion through her / his descriptions?

....

....

....

....

....

EXAM-STYLE QUESTION Q4 'In Night of the Scorpion' there is detailed description. Compare how description is used in this poem with how it is used in one other poem.

EXAM-STYLE QUESTION Q5 Description is sometimes used to recreate people or places. Choose a poem to link with "Presents from My Aunts..." and compare their use of description.

Metaphor

These Poems make strong use of Metaphor:

Limbo (pages 2-3)
Nothing's Changed (pages 4-6)
Blessing (pages 8-9)
Vultures (pages 14-15)
Search For My Tongue (pages 18-19)
Half-Caste (pages 22-23)
Love after Love (pages 24-25)
This Room (pages 26-27)

Q1 Why do you think poets sometimes choose to use a metaphor instead of describing something literally?

....

....

....

....

Q2 Sorry if this is getting a bit repetitive but I'm afraid that's just the way it is.
Select a poem from that box up there and explain why the poet's use of metaphors is effective.

....

....

....

....

....

Q3 Explain how the poet uses metaphor to create a particular impression in one of the other poems.

....

....

....

....

....

EXAM-STYLE QUESTION Q4 The use of metaphor in 'Vultures' is a powerful device. Compare how metaphors are used in 'Vultures' to one other poem from the Poems from Different Cultures.

EXAM-STYLE QUESTION Q5 'Half-Caste' uses metaphors to reinforce the poem's message. Find one other poem and compare how the two use metaphor to emphasise their different subjects.

Unusual Presentation

These Poems have Unusual Presentation:

Limbo (pages 2-3)
Nothing's Changed (pages 4-5)
Two Scavengers in a Truck... (pages 10-11)
What Were They Like? (pages 16-17)
Search For My Tongue (pages 18-19)
Unrelated Incidents (pages 20-21)
Presents from my Aunts in Pakistan (pages 28-29)

Q1 Why do you think a poet might decide to use an unusual style of presentation?

....

....

....

....

Q2 Explain what effect the style of presentation has in one of the poems that you are familiar with from the box above.

....

....

....

....

....

Q3 Now pick another poem. How does the unusual presentation reflect the poem's theme?

....

....

....

....

....

EXAM-STYLE QUESTION Q4 The unusual presentation of a poem often reflects the poet's ideas. Use 'Unrelated Incidents' and one other poem to demonstrate how the poets use this technique to support their ideas.

EXAM-STYLE QUESTION Q5 Compare the presentation of 'What Were They Like?' with one other poem which has unusual presentation from the Poems from Different Cultures.

Non-Standard English

These Poems use Non-Standard English:

Limbo (pages 2-3)
Island Man (pages 6-7)
Unrelated Incidents (pages 20-21)
Half-Caste (pages 22-23)

Q1 What is your understanding of "non-standard English"?

....

....

....

....

Q2 I imagine you've got the gist by now... choose a poem that you know from the top of the page. Why do you think the poet has chosen to write in non-standard English in this poem?

....

....

....

....

....

Q3 Now look at one of the other poems. How important is the style of language to the impact of the poem?

....

....

....

....

....

EXAM-STYLE QUESTION Q4 Language is an important part of our culture. 'Limbo' uses non-standard English to reinforce the ideas in the poem; find another poem that does this and compare them.

EXAM-STYLE QUESTION Q5 The way we speak is part of our culture. Compare the language used in 'Unrelated Incidents' to the language used in one other poem that uses non-standard English.

Particular Places

These Poems are about Particular Places:

Nothing's Changed (pages 4-5)
Island Man (pages 6-7)
Blessing (pages 8-9)
Two Scavengers in a Truck... (pages 10-11)
Vultures (pages 14-15)
What Were They Like? (16-17)
Presents from my Aunts in Pakistan (pages 28-29)
Hurricane Hits England (pages 32-33)

Q1 Write a couple of sentences to describe your favourite place.

....

....

....

....

Q2 Right, it's time to choose another poem from the blue box of destiny at the top of the page. What kind of image do we get of the place described in the poem?

....

....

....

....

....

Q3 Choose another poem. Why is the setting important to the impact of the poem?

....

....

....

....

....

EXAM-STYLE QUESTION Q4 Some poems, like 'Nothing's Changed', describe particular places. Compare 'Nothing's Changed' with one other poem which has a strong sense of place.

EXAM-STYLE QUESTION Q5 'Hurricane...' uses its description of a particular place to convey certain cultures. Choose another poem that uses this device and compare how effective the poems are at doing it.

Two Cultures

These Poems are about Two Cultures:

Island Man (pages 6-7)
Search For My Tongue (pages 18-19)
Unrelated Incidents (pages 20-21)
Half-Caste (pages 22-23)
Presents from my Aunts in Pakistan (pages 28-29)
Hurricane Hits England (pages 32-33)

Q1 Do you feel that you belong to just one culture, or to more than one?

Q2 Like you've done on every single page of this section, pick a poem that you've studied from the list above. Does the poet think that the two cultures can mix well or not? Explain your answer.

Q3 Select a second poem. How does this poet feel about cultures mixing together?

EXAM-STYLE QUESTION Q4 Comparing two distinct cultures can provide an effective contrast in a poem, such as in 'Island Man'. Compare how the two cultures are used in this and one other poem.

EXAM-STYLE QUESTION Q5 In 'Presents from My Aunts...' we are presented with a conflict between two cultures. Compare how this is portrayed, with a portrayal of conflicting cultures in one other poem.

Universal Ideas

These Poems are about Universal Ideas:

Nothing's Changed (pages 4-5)
Two Scavengers in a Truck... (pages 10-11)
Vultures (pages 14-15)
Half-Caste (pages 22-23)
Love After Love (pages 24-25)
This Room (pages 26-27)
Hurricane Hits England (pages 32-33)

Q1 Describe a film, TV programme, play or book that you have seen or read that made you think about a particular issue.

....

....

....

....

Q2 Pick a number from 1 to 7. Congratulations, you've just chosen a poem from the box at the top. What is the universal theme in this poem? How does the poet present this idea?

....

....

....

....

....

Q3 Another number, another poem. How is the situation described in this poem relevant to more general issues?

....

....

....

....

....

EXAM-STYLE QUESTION Q4 Many poets like their work to have universal ideas. Explain how the poets in 'Hurricane Hits England' and one other poem present their universal themes.

EXAM-STYLE QUESTION Q5 'Vultures' examines the universal idea of good and evil in mankind. Choose one other poem and compare how both poems present universal ideas.

Traditions

These Poems are about Traditions:

Limbo (pages 2-3)
Night of the Scorpion (pages 12-13)
What Were They Like? (pages 16-17)
Presents from my Aunts in Pakistan (pages 28-29)
Hurricane Hits England (pages 32-33)

Q1 Describe a tradition that you take part in.

Q2 OK, I promise this is the last time. Pick a poem from the box and explain what impression the poet gives of the traditions they describe.

Q3 Ooops, another question seems to have slipped in here, how did that happen?
Suppose you might as well do it now it's made the effort to come along.
Choose another poem. What is the effect of the poet's description of traditions in this poem?

EXAM-STYLE QUESTION Q4 'Night of the Scorpion' describes traditions which are becoming out-dated. Compare this with one other poem which uses the theme of tradition.

EXAM-STYLE QUESTION Q5 Traditions are essential ingredients of many cultures. Show how two poems refer to traditions to make their point. You must use 'Presents from My Aunts...' as one of your poems.

Acknowledgements

The Publisher would like to thank:

Chinua Achebe 'Vultures' from Collected Poems published by Carcanet reprinted by permission of David Higham Associates

Tatamkhulu Afrika 'Nothing's Changed' by Tatamkhulu Afrika from Night Rider: Selected Poems, published by Kwela Books

John Agard 'Half Caste' copyright © 1996 by John Agard reproduced by kind permission of John Agard c/o Caroline Sheldon Literary Agency Limited

Moniza Alvi *Carrying My Wife*, Bloodaxe Books, 2000

Sujata Bhatt 'Search for My Tongue' from *Brunizem* (1998), reprinted by permission of the publishers, Carcanet Press Ltd.

Edward Kamau Brathwaite 'Limbo' from *The Arrivants: A New World Trilogy* (OUP, 1973), reprinted by permission of Oxford University Press.

Imtiaz Dharker *Postcards from god*, Bloodaxe Books, 1997;
I Speak for the Devil, Bloodaxe Books 2001

Nissim Ezekiel 'Night of the Scorpion' from *Poverty Poems*, reproduced by permission of Oxford University Press India, New Delhi

Lawrence Ferlinghetti 'Two Scavengers in A Truck, Two Beautiful People in a Mercedes' By Lawrence Ferlinghetti, from *These are my rivers*, copyright © 1979 by Lawrence Ferlinghetti. Reprinted by permission of New Directions Publishing Corp

Tom Leonard 'Unrelated Incidents' © Tom Leonard, from *Intimate Voices* Etruscan Books, Devon

Denise Levertov 'What Were They Like?' from Selected Poems (Bloodaxe Books, 1986). Reproduced by permission of Pollinger Limited and the proprietor.

Grace Nichols 'Hurricane Hits England' Copyright © Grace Nichols 1996 reproduced with permission of Curtis Brown Group Ltd & 'Island Man' Copyright © Grace Nichols 1984 reproduced with permission of Curtis Brown Group Ltd

Niyi Osundare 'Not My Business' from Songs of the Seasons (Heinemann Educational Books, Nigeria, 1990)

Derek Walcott 'Love after Love' from *Sea Grapes* by Derek Walcott. Copyright © 1976 by Derek Walcott. Reprinted by permission of Farrar, Straus and Giroux, LLC.

Photographs:

'Children' With thanks to the District Six Museum

Every effort has been made to locate copyright holders and obtain permission to reproduce sources. For those sources where it has been difficult to trace the originator of the work, we would be grateful for information. If any copyright holder would like us to make an amendment to the acknowledgements, please notify us and we will gladly update the book at the next reprint. Thank you.